CALLED BY
DISTANCES

SOUTHERN MESSENGER POETS

Dave Smith, Series Editor

POEMS

CALLED BY DISTANCES

BILJANA D. OBRADOVIĆ

LOUISIANA STATE UNIVERSITY PRESS
BATON ROUGE

Published by Louisiana State University Press
lsupress.org

Copyright © 2026 by Biljana D. Obradović
All rights reserved. Except in the case of brief quotations used in articles or reviews, no part of this publication may be reproduced or transmitted in any format or by any means without written permission of Louisiana State University Press.

LSU Press Paperback Original

DESIGNER: Emily A. Olson
TYPEFACE: Arno Pro

Cover illustration: *My Private Diary—Blue,* by Meta Adamič Bahl. Courtesy of the artist.

CATALOGING-IN-PUBLICATION DATA ARE AVAILABLE FROM
THE LIBRARY OF CONGRESS.

ISBN 978-0-8071-8586-5 (paperback) | ISBN 978-0-8071-8597-1 (epub) | ISBN 978-0-8071-8598-8 (pdf)

for John and Petar

―

Ο πουζεις πατρις
(Where you live is where your country is)

—Old Greek saying

CONTENTS

Acknowledgments   ix

1. CALLED BY THE PAST

Rivers Run Through Me   3
An Alternate Journey   5
The Dream That Keeps Returning   6
Spiritual Baptism   7
My Yoga Class   8
Assimilation: How He Changed Her European Ways   10
Symmetry   11
Let's Eat Bread   13
Why I Can't Get Anything Done   15

2. CALLED BY LOVE & DEATH

September Broadway Ramblings, New Orleans   19
Stay Away from Construction Men   21
Waiting for Him   22
Pen Pals   24
All Cancers Are Brutal, But This One Is One of the Worst   27
Walk-In   28
The Mask: *Il Dottore, Il Medico Della Peste*   29
Wearing Black   32
Rape of K.R.   34

3. CALLED BY DISTANCES

First Bus Trip Through the USA   37
Pickled Snake in Wine   40

Ενοικιαζεται (For Rent)   41
A Greek Island Vacation   42
Taking Pictures in Des Moines   44
Mercury, "Friendship 7"   46
Traveling on a Train to Paris   47
Getting Ready for Parades   48
Carnival Time in New Orleans   50

4. CALLED BY NAMES

Ad Infinitum   55
Voting During My Lunch Break   57
Stories of My Name   58
A Hierarchy of Names   61
You Ugly!!!   63
Latrina's Lounge, Uptown New Orleans   65
Trendsetter: Or, How I Changed India   67
Catullus's Sparrows   68

5. CALLED BY NATURE

The Tamed West   73
Scenes at the Sheldon Art Gallery   75
Nature Unleashed   77
At the End of the Year in the Subtropics   79
Katrina: My "American Pie"   80
Raccoon in the Garbage   83
Waiting for Papayas   84
Yellow Water Lily   85

Notes   87

ACKNOWLEDGMENTS

Grateful acknowledgment is made to the editors of the following publications, in which some of these poems appeared previously (sometimes in slightly different versions):

Atlanta Review: "Trendsetter: Or, How I Changed India"; *Ezra Pound and Friendship: An Online Fusion of East and West:* "The Dream That Keeps Returning" (in English and Japanese, trans. Yoshiko Kita); *Journal of College Writing:* "An Alternate Journey"; *Ezra's Book,* ed. Justin Kishbaugh and Catherine E. Paul (Clemson University Press, 2019): "A Hierarchy of Names" and "Mercury, 'Friendship 7'"; *40th Anniversary of the Maple Leaf Poetry Readings: New Orleans, 1979–2019,* ed. John Travis (Portals Press, 2019): "Rivers Run Through Me"; *A Little Light from the Borders: Poems After Ezra Pound,* ed. Jeff Grieneisen and Rhett Forman (Clemson University Press, 2025): "A Greek Island Vacation," "My Yoga Class," "Symmetry," and "The Mask: *Il Dottore, Il Medico Della Peste*"; *Maple Leaf Rag VI: An Anthology of Poetic Writings,* ed. John Travis (Portals Press, 2017): "A Hierarchy of Names"; *A Packet of Poems for Ezra Pound,* ed. Catherine E. Paul and Justin Kishbaugh (Clemson University Press, 2018): "Pickled Snake in Wine"; *The Poetry Buffet: An Anthology of New Orleans Poetry,* ed. Gina Ferrara and Geoff Munsterman (New Orleans Poetry Journal Press, 2023): "Catullus's Sparrows."

―

Thanks go to the Department of English, Xavier University of Louisiana, Department Chair Dr. Oliver Hennessey, former Provost Dr. Anne McCall, and former Dean Dr. Camellia Okpodu for my Spring 2021 sabbatical, during which I was able to complete this book. Special thanks to John Gery, Tim

Skeen, Pam Weiner, Hannah Baker Saltmarsh, Alan Gravano, Jeremy Tuman, Anya Groner, Bart Everson, and editor Dave Smith, for valuable suggestions as well as to Vesna and the late Zoran Kilibarda, Tamara Malešev, Robert Boo, Elza Ivović Holt, Nicole Greene, Paulina and the late Vlajko Kocić, Michele and Mel Levy, and to my family, John and Petar Gery, for their support.

1
CALLED BY THE PAST

Rivers Run Through Me

       for Katherine Nelson-Born

I.

In New Orleans, I offer my friend water. "I grew up poor,
starving, even homeless," she says. "We couldn't pay
the water bill." Now, still thin, she says, "You eat a lot
later in life, or forget to eat." She gulps the bright water.

I tell her I need to lose twenty pounds. Her sister goes
on frequent food-shopping sprees afraid of hunger at home.
I tell her in the Customs House, our home by the Danube
across from Bulgaria in Yugoslavia, we had no running water.

My mother carried buckets of water three flights of stairs
to cook, wash our clothes, wash our bodies,
to wash away the excrement in our bathroom.
We ate a lot of Serbian bean soup, sometimes sour cabbage

with my grandmother's ham and whole chickens on potatoes.
But across from the phosphate factory that made detergent
for laundry and agricultural fertilizer—a stinking nightmare—
we couldn't afford to eat chicken and potatoes every Sunday.

We played at writing on dust on our coffee table
each day with the chemical that had entered
our old apartment house through the wall cracks.
My father, who saw this would kill us and his employees,

as manager of the Customs House, demanded the factory
give us new apartments and clean water, or be sued.
They listened. The factory and the river hummed on.
My father and mother both died of cancer at age sixty-six.

II.

Forty years later, friends drove me to see Prahovo,
where we had lived in the middle of nowhere,
its gray damp walls, near the main part of that village.
I passed my old school. I didn't remember it at all.

Today I recall the long walks in the snow there and back,
nothing in between except the river and wolves howling.
I knocked on our old apartment door to see who was home.
Would she know me? No. An old lady who lives there now

opened the door. She let me in to look. In her sink still
no running water—half a century and no one has fixed it.
Powder, grit from the same factory dusted her table.
She warned me snakes live in the unused backyard.

When the old lady asked me to sit down, she offered me
preserves she had made and a glass of cold water.
I thanked her, but didn't want any, afraid of what she
must have borne for years up dirty stairs, like my mother.

But through a bedroom window I could glimpse the blue,
beautiful Danube. So I gulped the gray water she gave me,
her hand trembling. No wonder rivers run through me,
the life I have lived, the Danube then, now the Mississippi.

An Alternate Journey

When people come to meet us the first time
        they are surprised to see so many shelves
filled with books, no flat-screen TV. In their homes,
        I imagine, no bookshelves, just blank
walls, priceless paintings. Are we so poor? They must

revel in their gigantic palaces, two-car garages,
        bright, huge BMW SUVs, or worse,
one of those tank-like guzzlers, a Hummer
        (whose production, thank God, has stopped)
they drive into nature. What a life! On their porches

gas barbeque grills fire thick filet mignon
        served on Delft plates. No wonder
they need their exercise machines, as they pile on
        dollars and pounds, always counting. At home
the sleek TV reruns show images of places they seek.

In winter, they doze through cruises to the Virgin Islands,
        dining on fresh lobster and crab.
In their Apple earbuds streams smooth, steady
        jazz—a little Stan Getz maybe, but
(I wouldn't be surprised) Dolly Parton.

I never planned getting rich, when cheap
        books filled my room with dreams.
Young, I wanted to find my way
        to the world where the poems
of Frost I read would lead me to some warm

forest infested with pesky mosquitoes. I didn't want to wait
        for money to show me the way. Poor,
I'd choose my brother's chapbooks for my Trailways
        bus tour across the Wild West.
Words under pressure, I thought, take small risks, too.

The Dream That Keeps Returning

       Bombay, India

At teatime by the fountain in front of Breach Candy
Club, abandoned leather gloves lie in a convertible,
their owner, unlike me, a known British aristocrat.
I browse through *The Times of India* under shade.

It's too hot to eat, but my stomach protests,
my eyes instantly catch the *bera*'s attention.
I whistle lightly and he hurries, bows,
handing me the menu, as if for the first time.

I ask for a chicken *biryani,* identical to the dish my neighbor
just polished off, leaving only crumbs of a baguette
cut up in a little cane basket. I return the laminated menu,
ask for an iced tea, to cool the chaos in my head.

My ego suffers. I want to lead. I want this man
to know who I am, but also I like my silence, my peace.
I need a platform from which to speak, be heard.
I want him to hear me. Where is he?

How can he leave his gentle gloves unattended,
so that any beggar in search of *baksheesh* can steal them,
possess him, when I cannot? My mind—a jigsaw puzzle,
with its pieces, as if bread, strewn all over the grass

where iguanas' long tails stretch. Their tongues are far
in front, ready to attack, eat the flies around them.
They blend with the ground, hidden as baguette crumbs.
I can't hide. I don't blend. May my *biryani* help.

Spiritual Baptism

Today I gave up my resolution to be baptized
after a cup of French vanilla with an Orthodox minister;
I just can't believe, but I still sat with him, talked.

Would my gray hairs darken from baptismal water
or would they become even grayer, whiter?
I was raised to hate faith, but not the spirit.

Have centaurs come out of mating a horse and a man?
Lost in my sneeze, I ask, stare at an ancient Greek vase,
a mere replica, my line of sight drifting to the floor.

After watching Mumbai's TV news today, my friend thinks
it was a lover who stabbed a sixteen-year-old imprisoned murderer.
So much gay jealousy, such wickedness, he smiles.

In only twelve years the population of the former Bombay,
grown by five million people—I still want to go back,
visit the old hangouts, walk on Chowpatty Beach

as I did on Ganesh's holiday with Phillipe, a French friend,
when the mob nearly stole his camera—drunks,
feverish with religious festivities, splashing us.

I've never seen the photos he took of me then.
What did I look like? Did he manage to catch
only my body and the elephant statue for my head?

I told the priest how people threw me in the waves
where I melted like the soft Ganesh figurines, the Arabian
Sea polluting what little spirit I had in me even then.

My Yoga Class

      for Laura Flora, my yogini

Laura starts by giving out Mexican blankets to sit on,
then purple blocks and belts, as we unroll our mats, remove
our watches, place our water bottles like talismans on the ground.

When all sixteen women (no men today)
are cross-legged, she begins. Her theme today,
"What are we thankful for, or should we be?"

This for November, the Thanksgiving month.
So each day she tells people what she's thankful for
—for simple things, food on the table, shelter,

electricity, or water, for the people around us each day.
I half-listen. I don't like sermons. I don't want to be in church.
I don't want someone tell me what to do.

While she speaks, I have to move my legs, already achy
from this pose on the mat (and we haven't even started yet!).
Even with the blanket underneath for support, my sacrum

(which she has realigned herself so many times) hurts.
I am afraid to ask her to do it again as she always comments,
if she were a chiropractor, she would have been rich.

She has given me names of chiropractors, but I don't call them.
After three rounds of Om, listening to each other breathing
we begin with increasing intensity: from child to down dog

to warrior, to pigeon, to whatever end pose she has devised
for the part of the body we're concentrating on today—the core?
After an hour or more, another quiet rest on our backs, *shavasana*—

which she breaks with a ceremonial ringing of small bells—
we say Om once more then quit, and I drag myself past
people meditating over Bloody Marys at the Ruby Slipper.

Assimilation: How He Changed
Her European Ways

    for John

He liked tapioca pudding for dessert when
they first started dating. He made it for her,
then she for him. When she visited her family
over Christmas break, he bought her
a coffee machine, for him, really, to have
American coffee instead of instant coffee
each morning she was used to on her own.

He taught her to prepare inexpensive food
out of a can, salmon burgers she then made
often for them. He taught her to make
Mexican food with ground beef or with
shredded chicken and pinto beans in a tortilla—
sour cream, black olives, tomatoes,
lettuce, guacamole, and yes, salsa.

He taught her to toss Chinese food in a wok—
vegetables chopped up, bamboo shoots
with sliced water chestnuts (which she had never
eaten before). They had eggs with potatoes
and ham or kielbasa for Sunday brunch
mostly Sunny Side Up, that she liked, that
reminded her of her grandmother's farm eggs,
but on special occasions eventually he'd

make Eggs Benedict, though he never taught her
how to make them. His secret recipe, he'd say.
She didn't want to learn, wanted him to make them.
She was only the sous-chef who prepared the Hollandaise
from scratch, sliced the tomatoes, English muffins,
then heated the Canadian bacon. However, he insisted she
cut a sprig of parsley from her herb garden for garnish.

Symmetry

We arrive at the train station, excited
about our return to Venezia,
but instead, after the short walk, are startled.
At Hotel Basilea, the desk clerk Marco
tells us what seems nobody's business,
chatting with my husband and me.
Two summers have passed since
he's seen us. For fifteen years
we've come every or every other year,
regulars enough to confide in us.
He says that his love life is so bad
even if he threw himself off
the Rialto Bridge, no one would care.

The glass chandelier on our large
palazzo-like room's ceiling is asymmetrical:
five balls of light, but between
two of them there is too much space,
more than between the other lights.
We are used to the spaces between balls
being exactly the same.
At this, not a mass-produced chandelier—
a beautiful, expensive, hand-blown,
a Murano glass piece, with brown and
light-yellow, almost gold-colored glass,
and ornamental leaves and flowers,
we cannot stop looking.

My husband and I wonder, what if someone
were to knock it with a long umbrella,
break it accidentally? We won't.
We are careful, but also obsessed.
It bothers us. Why did the artist
make it asymmetrical? For what purpose?

A mistake? We yearn for symmetry.
We look up, like Marco not being in love—
surprised when we lack love, we suffer,
we crave, and repeat odd things helplessly.

Let's Eat Bread

Grandma used to say, "Let's eat bread," meaning
let's eat, have lunch, or dinner. With every
dish she'd make—like stuffed peppers—we would
cut a slice or two of her country sourdough.

When I was a kid, she'd bake the bread in the fireplace,
in a clay pot in hot embers. When she pulled out
the huge round bread, she would cut a long slice
and put lard with paprika and salt on it.

The pig fat would melt into the bread.
Often she would also make small round rolls
called *kravajčići,* like Kaiser rolls.
At Easter she'd put a whole egg on top,

or knead the dough into little geese. Some
mornings she'd bake a *pogača,* a flatbread, which
apparently shares its name with *focaccia,* poked with a fork,
something I've never tasted anywhere since.

In the U.S. supermarkets or bakeries, I can't find
bread that comes even close to the grocery bread
back home, or if I do, it tends to be overpriced,
like sourdough, or flaxseed bread—*pane al lino.*

And so, I don't eat bread often anymore.
If I have potatoes, rice, or pasta, I don't eat bread.
Although for lunch, I love a good slice
with margarine and some *kasseri* cheese.

Never have I made my own bread.
When we got married all I wanted was
a bread machine as a gift. But we registered too late,
so never got one. I am still waiting.

Of course, Grandma didn't use a machine.
Once a week, she'd knead the flour, yeast, water . . .
let it rise. Then sit and watch it bake in the oven.
Why shouldn't I use my hands instead of a machine?

Why I Can't Get Anything Done

While I was at the library, I couldn't find my keys.
I hoped I hadn't left them in my Volkswagen car,
But I had, so I called a locksmith; the man
Came, opened my car door. I could then get back into the house.
"There," he said. I found the second set, by the mouse
Perched on *Women Get Something Done*, the book

I've been reading forever, my unfinished book!
Then I had to pay the man who helped me find my keys.
But as I went toward them, I watched the mouse
Pass me, out the door, up a tire, into my car.
"At last, one nasty creature out of my house!"
"Maybe he wants to drive your car," joked the man.

He grinned. "I don't do cars, but Jack does, your pest man."
Then he left. I had to go so wrote in my notebook:
Remember to call pest man! when back at the house.
Had I paid the key man? Yes, so I grabbed my keys,
Lifted my purse, and raced to the library in my car.
But when I returned home, I noticed my mouse

Lingering on the sidewalk. I felt besieged by the mouse,
Violated. I waved across the street to an old man,
My neighbor. He ignored me. Took off in his car.
What should I do? Like the mouse paging through my book,
I thought I can wait or do something. Using keys,
I killed the engine, then walked slowly to my house.

I remembered the alarm code to get into my house,
But then thought to call Jack about the mouse.
Opening my purse and also the door with my keys,
The alarm blared and blasted! Now I needed the man
Whose phone number hid in my god-knows-where book
Of addresses. Nobody could help me. Maybe in the car?

I went outside, again, like a lunatic, and unlocked the car,
Scared I would fail, scared I'd never get in my house
Again in a dark corner, like a cat asleep, lay the book
That disarmed the noise, with Jack who'd kill my mouse
ASAP. "But Lady," he said like any workman,
"It'll be next week, maybe longer." All I had left was keys,

And my car that always started, like hope in unread books
Where people get things done, like a mouse in a dream
In *Of Mice and Men,* where I'd find the key. In my house.

CALLED BY LOVE & DEATH

2

September Broadway Ramblings, New Orleans

"Bubba's Best Produce in the South" truck passes by on Broadway
just past noon while I smoke another cigarette alone on the porch
among our plants, minus the one palm I noticed someone stole
yesterday, the day we changed a light bulb for Greg's silver birthday,
his twenty-sixth, on the last lunar eclipse of this century
(the earlier one was in '68). On the steps, friends smoked a joint,
emptied the Abita Amber keg, and ate chocolate cherry cake.

Tonight we'll revisit Molly's at the Market, greet the red-haired waitress
whose boyfriend last week committed suicide in front of her, then
ask what happened to the Jesus-bearded man bumming cigarettes
at the window, who was asked a second time to stop disturbing us,
then arrested. Cops came in flocks. Handcuffed at the back, he nodded
as he passed Molly's window again. Another time Karl, a ship chandler,
who bought us a round to stare at me, I think, named all the Quarter streets,

recounting the history behind each name, even how he had to shoot a mugger,
hurting him, who later died. Although every morning he wakes up
seeing the dead man's face, he's not sorry he killed him. He's sorry
for the man's momma. Saturday we might go to Buddha Belly Burger Bar,
drink some Igor's, watch the Saints, while Mark and Eric do laundry.
I'll watch TV, do my laundry, too—washers, dryers—then return
to the bar, going off-screen, from the closed-circuit TV watching us.

Last week, we met Igor at his Garlic Clove, chatted with his wife,
and found out he came from Rijeka, when it was still Fiume. Italian-Croatian.
Besides the Belly, he also owns Igor's, Check-Point Charlie's, the Clove
where we play pool. Kids from nearby hostels do their laundry, just off
planes from Melbourne or wherever. Usually, I find someone to play foosball,
eager for a challenge, usually beat him. (As a student in Lincoln, I played
Thanksgiving games with poet Greg Kuzma and his son, Mark, learning.)

To get home, we catch the St. Charles streetcar to Napoleon, Mark
and Eric's, then Constance, then by the Club. At last, in front of their house,

we spot cats Gandhi and Blake, frothing at the mouth from flea spray.
A neighbor's baby screams. Inside, red lights, multicolored
candles soothe the soul, R.E.M. revives. I sip a cooled Chardonnay. The heat
and humidity may subside, as they say, but we can't imagine
real cool. We're temporary residents. Meanwhile, we watch mud-slinging,

shouting, "I want a Moral President—NOT CLINTON." Mark talks
to a woman involved in a catfight. Two arrests this week near us.
Only one plant stolen. Art's head is smashed by a gay man, a metal pipe,
convinced Art and G. were FBI agents harassing gays. Birds chirp.
On CNN, Israelis open a tunnel under a mosque, Palestinians scream.
In Serbia, the UN lifts all sanctions after Dayton. End to suffering? But, I'm in
New Orleans. Take me home. Take me home, where Buddhas or buffaloes roam.

Stay Away from Construction Men

A man stands inside a red, white, and blue dumpster,
a scarf covering his head, glasses his eyes and another covering
his face. Frankly I'm scared of him. As I approach
on the sidewalk, I nod as if to say, "Hi, I'm just passing by.
Don't hurt me." He nods back. I pass, thinking it's the end,
but instead, he says, "Oh, I was trying to flirt with you.
That's what construction workers love doing, you know?"

I half-listen, walk away, nod again—now furious.
So here is my response, Mr. Construction Man.
I'm a professor at a university where I teach young women
to stay away from guys like you by getting an education.
If you had one yourself, you'd actually be able to remove
your red bandannas and walk the street liberated just as I am.
So, if you should see this lady again, do not nod or say anything.

Waiting for Him

>for M.

I have been waiting for my boyfriend for two hours. Hours
>or is it years now? I'm uncertain he will arrive. Where is he?
Dressed in black, as if mourning, he might as well be gone already,
>even though he hasn't arrived yet.

Perhaps his roommate's bike wouldn't start, or he ran out of gas,
>or he decided to get on the St. Charles streetcar
and the driver kept waving to his sisters, cousins, aunts . . .
>ringing the bell, stalling—chatting with a cop.

I know he had to feed his cats, Blake and G.,
>who must've jumped on him the minute he set foot inside;
their neighbors, Squeaky and yellow cat,
>may have also smelled the feast.

Every day he tells me this may be his last. Unconvinced,
>I wait in silence, keeping my distance,
to give him space. I want to call, but his answering machine
>picks up. His phone is always off. I am a burden.

He claims he can't even take care of himself, let alone me,
>his problems overwhelming. He hates getting up at dawn,
despises teaching students who don't understand, or seem
>deaf, yet he doesn't earn enough to subsist.

When his Santa Barbara house burnt to the ground, he lost everything,
>even baseball caps, T-shirts. His "friends" don't care.
John, his best friend, died. Nancy, his love of nine years,
>left him for a heroin addict. He still sleeps around.

When he is missing the past, he drowns his pain in whiskey sours,
        and thinks of moving. I try to find him. Call him, but
he can't hear me calling him. His loud music, usually R.E.M.,
        drowns outside sounds, as if to shake the world

away, yet it's still here. I am out there, waiting for him. Come back—
        let death blow past us in the summer breeze,
stand in the first yellowing of leaves, the winter mist. I beg him.
        Open. Smell the spring. Lily-of-the-valley.

Pen Pals

    for Bob

I.

In 1970, in Salonika, in the American school
I was given a task in fifth grade to write a letter
to a pen pal, a boy from Westville, Indiana,
named Bob who, I found out later, liked to play volleyball,
read Michener and like me Elizabeth Barrett Browning;
it was a hard task for a nine-year-old Serbian girl,

who had almost no English skills. But I wrote Bob,
who wrote back, wherever I happened to be: Belgrade,
Salonika, or Bombay—back and forth for month after month,
for eighteen years! He sent me photos of himself. I sent mine.
He sent me a tape with his voice, his favorite music—
Barbara Streisand's "Evergreen" and "Memories"...

Oh, listening to this romantic tape, how I dreamt,
how I hoped to meet him one day, wearing the same Purdue Snoopy
T-shirt he'd sent me; how I dreamt, one day we would wed.
America was far away! I satisfied myself by cooking
from his gourmet recipes. When a decade later I came to the U.S.,
as if by a miracle, I found him through a Chicago phone operator.

Who else would have his last name! Not knowing what
to say, I dialed. But, luckily, the answering machine was on
and I recognized the voice from his tape. So, I left a message.
The next day for the first time, Chicago to Richmond, we talked.
He asked me to come see him, spend my winter break.
On a cold January 3rd, 1989, at O'Hare: I held up a sign—

"Pen Pal from Yugoslavia Meets Her Pen Pal After 18 Years!"
Would he recognize me? A tall, blond, hunk of a man
in a three-piece suit walked toward me, gave me a bear hug, a kiss.

He laughed his laugh I'd recognize anywhere.
He showed me Chicago, its Sears Tower, the Art Institute,
restaurants, bars, cafes, and made for me the most wonderful party

where I met all his gay friends. He showed me off.
He told me so many things I didn't know—he was afraid
I might not accept him for who he was—a gay man.
He loved my stylish clothes, fancy shoes, and scarves.
He met my brother in New York. I met more of his friends.
Some are gone now from AIDS, some still ailing, some were saved.

II.

Oh, the Miss Volleyball Pageant, the Chicago stripper dance
when I stuck a dollar bill in a "cop's" G-string. "What a hoot!"
he would say. All the fun, the laughter, the little secrets.
And the now dearly departed Coco, dog, I'd walk around Irving Park.
Then my long train ride from my Lincoln to his New Orleans, the jazz,
Huckleberry Finn–like ride during the floods of '93, the Absinthe Bar,

Mark Twain's favorite, the blues, the shrimp and gumbo,
the great-plantation tour, meeting his parents for the first time
in his great 1850 house. Oh, the great brass bed!
The water volleyball games, daiquiris, and jambalaya . . .
The Fourth of July Houston and Galveston, Texas, trip.
Visiting his old friend from Westville who had stopped writing

to his own pen pal from my class—my best friend.
The great barbequed Texas steaks, the oil wells . . .
The space ice cream for the astronauts at the Houston Space Center,
Mission Control from where I'd seen the first man on the moon.
The Gulf of Mexico swim. I met his parents (now both dead),
his four brothers, nieces before we decided to move in together.

III.

In our 1932 Broadway house, he later found out at nineteen he had fathered
a daughter, now had grandkids. (So, we could have had our own kid.)
Now happily married to a man in Miami, he lives near the beach.
Fifty-four years of friendship, ours longer than many marriages.
"We Never Really Say Good-Bye," we'll sing together again,
as sung on his tape, my dearest B., my friend, my pen pal, forever.

All Cancers Are Brutal, But This One Is One of the Worst

The other day a friend told me of someone's illness.
I had no idea that our mutual friend had cancer.
So I wrote to him, asked him how he was,
only to find out he's been sick all year.

I had no idea this good friend had cancer,
bladder cancer (I had never heard of before),
only to find out he's been sick all year
and has had six different treatments.

Bladder cancer (I had never heard of before)
is especially difficult for male patients
and he's had as many as six treatments.
What was I supposed to do—pretend I'd never heard?

It's especially difficult for male patients,
so I wrote to him, asked him how he was.
What was I supposed to do—pretend I'd only heard
the other day a friend telling me of someone's illness?

Walk-In

      Lewisburg, PA

The first salon I walked in was empty, yet they wouldn't cut my hair—no walk-ins.
Pushing my son in his stroller, I went to a second, on Market Street a block away.
After the hairdresser washed my hair, began trimming, she said, "I look awful today.
I'm sorry. My niece died this morning at 4:00 a.m., cancer, left a four-year-old daughter.
Her grandmother will raise her, I guess. The girl's father is hopeless.

She wanted to die at home and, before she did, the whole night we heard strange
noises. Then just before she died, her daughter woke up, as if she knew,
the strangest thing." Her coworker came in, bringing the hairdresser lunch
and a consoling hug. She must've taken me on her lunch break—better to work
than to think. "You didn't know you'd hear this when you walked in, did you?"

Being a walk-in has its costs. I tried to console her, and thank her for taking me in.
Both my parents died of cancer within six months of each other. I knew
what she was feeling, stunned. Still, they were older than this young woman.
I was patient, careful not to tell her how the last hairdresser ruined my hair,
one side shorter than the other. Who knows if she would concentrate

with so much death on her mind. Perhaps I should have waited, but
I really needed a cut. In the end I gave her a nice tip. I had to.
I offered my condolences, not a nice day, which obviously she wouldn't have.
At the store to buy postcards, with my child, waiting for the cashier, I watched
an old man pass. Stalled as if to answer something someone asked, out

of the blue the cashier said, "The cancer's got him; days are numbered.
He just walks in and we take care of him." "A shame," I said.
I thought about my mom's hair falling out. He held the door wide so I might not
wake my baby son in the stroller, following the old man. I walked out with him,
letting my hair sway down the block on Market Street, each caring for the other.

The Mask: *Il Dottore,*
Il Medico Della Peste

I. Venice, Italy, 1998

The beaklike, bespectacled, papier-mâché,
white and black mask I carried onto the plane
from Venice across the pond
has been collecting dust, hanging
on our living room wall for years.
I bought the traditional mask of the plague-

doctor found at a specialized *Carnivale* store.
Venice, the city where my husband
and I have been going each summer,
has a special place in our hearts.
But instead of proposing in an osteria in Venice,
when the time came, when it was necessary

(we'd been trying to get pregnant and I did),
he proposed at Venezia, a pizza and pasta
place, in Mid-City, New Orleans,
where people also wear masks
to celebrate Mardi Gras. But, in Venice
he never wanted to ride in a gondola

until I managed to persuade him at last;
two years later, the gondola ride happened.
It was far too expensive to ride on our own.
So, we went with his students, a couple,
and our two-year-old baby son—
not very romantic—neither were

the arias the gondolier sang, too touristy,
yet going down narrow canals at sunset
with the red and yellow sun reflecting
against the palazzos, still seemed magical,

so that one would have wanted to kiss.
Alas, we didn't. Maybe he was too shy

(needed a mask!), in front of his students.
The next summer on the way to the airport in
a water taxi, predawn, the light was beautiful,
then the sky opened, the pelting rain kissed my cheeks,
lightning nearly struck the boat so it almost capsized;
we nearly lost our baby, the stroller, all sixteen suitcases.

II. Covid-19, New Orleans, 2020

I never imagined we'd need this mask.
Suddenly, during the Covid pandemic,
we had to wear masks, not for romance,
but to protect ourselves from the invisible.
The old plague-doctor mask reminded me of what
my parents had brought from India, peacock

feathers, beautiful—green and purple—sign
of good fortune. But someone said no,
remove them because they bring bad luck.
(My parents both died of cancer.) What
should we do with romance, destroy it?
The ancient ones knew the value of masks,

protection from bad smells, from plague,
death, sorrow, *dottores* donning masks with
lavender (sweet-smelling), roses, carnations, herbs.
They wore gloves, boots, drooping black capes
and wide-brimmed hats. Only with wooden
canes did they take off clothes, touching bodies

with the end of their long sticks.
In 1656 half a million people in Rome,
in Naples died. Those left behind, terrified
by doctors in costume and dying loved ones,
understood how beauty and fear married
in masks, so saved them to save the future.

Our masks did not save millions. Covid
killed them, but when putting on
the plague-doctor mask or Covid mask,
we think of half-faces looking at us.
Doctors don clear plastic shield-masks, and
we see again how easily horror comes.

We have nightmares of peacock feathers
and lavender. We try to talk as we once did,
lovingly, but some words get broken,
some are buried. Still with masks on
(although some are saying, "Take them off!"),
we go on, while the mask stares at us from the wall.

Wearing Black

1999

On New Year's Day, I mourn
my mother, dead, gone,
finished...at the beginning,
almost a new millennium.

Should I wear black clothes
for my mother, show I mourn?
Black for death, the ground,
night, darkness, sadness?

All my clothes have to be black—
I had promised her to wear them
as she had for her mother, her father
for 40 days, 40 nights, up to a year.

But, in America, you don't see mourners
in black clothes, without makeup.
Anyway, I used to wear black
before now, so who will know?

Should I wear a black armband
or black scarf on my head
to show I am in mourning
and wish to be exempted from joy?

No one's here to help me
with this ritual. Instead,
my colleague suggested
I see a psychologist, hers.

As a new American I noticed
even Roosevelt wore a black armband
to mourn his mother. A photo
of Sherman shows a black ribbon

on him after Lincoln's assassination.
Like these famous people,
should I wear black for death?
I don't know the rules here.

Or should I go on without?
My mother is dead anyway,
not around to see if I have paid
my respect. But I am not in Belgrade

to visit her grave each day of
those 40 days, to bring her fresh flowers,
to light the wax candles. Here,
I must find my own way to mourn.

Rape of K.R.

He sure was dressed like a beautiful black swan today in court.
Who would've thought he was anything but the devil in disguise
as a sleek swan! In court in a spotless suit, clean shoes, even
a square in his suit pocket, his dark-rimmed glasses made
him an intellectual. He was anything but that.

He never finished high school, by twenty-two had fathered two
children with his absent "baby mommas," but had never married.
He lost number one. He left his second baby momma
on the street, amid Friday Mardi Gras madness on Bourbon Street,
six months pregnant in high heels, to cruise around,

even after she had asked him to take her home. Disguised as
an Uber driver, he picked up K., trying to go back to her hotel,
get some rest, no baby momma. He took her to a dark street in the Marigny,
after showing her his silver gun, forced her to have sex with him,
then threatening her things could get worse. What? This was not enough?

Would he kill her, too? Well, he might as well have killed her.
Thank god for the emergency room abortion pill (which you could buy then),
she would not have to deliver a Helen, nor become his third
baby momma. She couldn't fight him off. Which woman can?
He is no god, no Zeus. Today, we laid a judgment on him. Listen:

He will spend the rest of his life in prison, never allowed out.
His two kids will have no father. His mother, who sat in court
supporting her son today, may regret she had not raised him properly.
(No sign of his own father.) And the sobbing girl K. can leave.
One of six women jurors, I watched, I never dreamed in my life

I would have to go through such a thing like rape, close up,
not like the movies or TV we watch with beer. Now I must live
with this every day, forced to make a judgment in
an imperfect world for a sobbing girl who will bear the burden.
Right and wrong, like old memories, getting in a car with a stranger.

3
CALLED BY DISTANCES

First Bus Trip Through the USA

> for Greg Donovan, March 1988

On my first trip through the USA,
thirty years ago by Greyhound bus
Tampa, Florida, to Richmond,
I had no clue what kind of people
travelled by bus, so I took the chance,
thinking all classes of people go by bus,

as in Europe. Throughout the night.
a man kept screaming profanities
like "fuck," and "assholes."
He wouldn't stop even though warned,
even though people of all ages
surrounded him, including little children.

I was used to that kind of a thing;
it didn't bother me, as it did others,
except I couldn't get much sleep.
The driver decided to do something, make
an unscheduled stop, and ask the man
to come to the front, to come out.

The man took the microphone,
yelled more profanities, explaining
he was from New York City
(as if that was his excuse).
Thus he sealed his fate, having
had had enough, the bus driver

dragged the man down the bus steps,
and hit him in the face, maybe
even breaking his nose.
Soon the police officers arrived.

They cuffed the man, arresting him
for unruly conduct in a public place.

The cop passed out a form to us,
"Remember to fill out your exact
seats when the incident occurred,"
they said. (This sort of thing must
happen often.) Then asked if we agreed
with the bus driver's actions.

But, I felt uncomfortable
making a statement. The man
was offensive, but not enough
to be punched and arrested.
He hadn't bothered me
personally, or anyone else.

Who knows what was going on!
Maybe he'd just lost his only son,
or his mother. Maybe he was drunk
or on drugs, bent on making trouble.
In the end, I don't remember
what I wrote. But I had to leave

an address in case they needed
to bring me to court as a witness.
What would be the chance of my
coming from Yugoslavia as a witness?
But you never know. Before I left,
two months earlier at home,

my aunt had warned my mother
about sending her only daughter to
"that violent Wild West country. Who knows

what could happen to her there," she said,
"They all own guns and are violent,"
but my mother still wanted me to go.

In Richmond, my future mentor
picked me up. He'd bring me
to study in the States. At 4:00 a.m. it was
too early to take me to his place to meet
his girlfriend, for coffee. Instead, he took me
at sunrise to Church Hill where we looked

across the flickering lights of the city
and to his surprise, I uttered the words
I already knew from American history,
which Patrick Henry had said there long ago,
"Give me liberty or give me death."
I knew this was a land I'd like to live in.

Pickled Snake in Wine

       in memory of Dragoslav Obradović

We all knew about my father's hatred and fear of snakes.
He wouldn't even look at a picture of one, let alone
at a live one in a zoo, or one on TV in a nature show.

I, too, am terrified of snakes. But not my brother,
nor my son. Later my husband, not I, took our son
to look at them at the New Orleans Audubon Zoo.

But the most extreme example of my father's phobia
occurred when he went on a Far East diplomatic mail pickup trip.
A colleague who had once lived there asked him to bring back wine

with "a pickled snake for virility," for better sexual performance.
Due to high alcohol content, it's drunk from a shot glass.
Dad bought a bottle in China, but couldn't sleep.

His hotel room glowed with the snake's presence in his suitcase.
After he returned, he showed it to us, then called his friend,
pleading with him to come and take it away. He refused to drink

what the man offered to him, especially not after his joke
that after drinking the wine, he'd chop up the snake and eat it too.
My mother, who knew what a thing fear can be, laughed the hardest.
"Take it away," my father shouted. "Yes, do," my mother sighed.

Ενοικιαζεται (For Rent)

So many stores are closed in Thessaloniki, my once home
away from home—offices, restaurants, shoe shops, bakeries,
boutiques. Just walk down Tsimiski Street now, you'll see.
Forced to close shops even around Aristotelous Square,
forced to lay off so many Greeks. Many of my friends,
even, have been laid off, with only months
left of their savings. Will they make it?

In two weeks, the election will determine it:
will the drachma replace the euro? Will
communists take over and nationalize the banks,
the τράπεζες, providing six years of unemployment coverage,
as if such promise is even possible? So says my friend
I haven't seen in twenty-four years, our reunion
bleak in this political house of cards.

One after the other they fall—jobs lost, futures
uncertain. Must they return to the places
far away their parents left, twentieth-century orphans,
to have better lives? Too old to move their
families (as their parents had) back to Australia, Panama,
the U.S., to begin again, but their kids may need to.
Yet has life also changed in those faraway places?

In these street faces I see the same despair of my own family's fortune.
I may never be able to return with my own son to this
paradiso terrestre, these olive groves, these orange-lined streets,
now covered in graffiti by young, frustrated men,
who choose now to desecrate these heroic Greek statues,
standing guard (regardless of graffiti) over a glorious golden age,
this biblical city that Saint Paul considered, as I did, a home.

A Greek Island Vacation

>   for my brother, Bata

I.

By Ipsos town on Corfu, the sea is clear
clean, an aqua temple for tourists ready
for rest, for swimming, for eating *souvlaki*.

New patrons arrive each Saturday by ferry from
the east, the Greek mainland, or the west, Italy.
As they walk this ground, do they understand

Odysseus may have stepped where they step.
They swim, tan, eat some octopus or a gyro wrap,
then drink Ouzo. When they tire of the sea,

they go into Kerkyra, to shoe-shop
just because . . . or wander through Orthodox churches,
or take a tour of the forts, old and new,

one built by Venetians, the other by Englishmen.
They gaze where the Durrell brothers played and wrote
travel pieces, with lots of male cicadas chirping,

attracting the female ones to mate, *tzitzikas*.
Now I hear them at night, all the time, everywhere,
their music making you hungry, waking you up.

Some introspective types even take a drive
uphill for a tour of Achilleion Palace, beyond the blue
water where infinity starts, but they love most

the villa owned by much-beloved Elizabeth, Austro-
Hungarian queen. Imagine the elaborate balls
held there, unseen by the island below.

II.

I take my son on a small boat ride across
from the main city, to the island of Vido, to see
where a hundred years ago Serbian soldiers

debarked, fleeing the German army,
walking for weeks with torn shoes or barefoot,
starving, in the middle of winter through snow.

After contracting typhoid, they landed on Ipsos
where we have come to swim. Thousands got sick,
and died on this desolate island, once a hospital,

now a tomb with their names lined up, divisions
identified, their hometowns. We start to search
for a grand-uncle who may have died here

long ago. But now time is short. We remember,
then cruise to see other little towns, dive through caves,
buy local olive carvings, kumquat liquor, candies,

jam this land sweetens, obligatory souvenirs, before escaping
back to our lives wanting it all, hands full of new perspectives,
but we never find my grand-uncle's name.

Taking Pictures in Des Moines

Lately I have no desire to take pictures,
to capture the present for posterity,
to make images of my life here to keep at home,
for those far away, but dear to my heart.

This new move desensitizing, this city, its people—dull.
It's been three months since my friends drove a truck
with my things. No one visits for coffee. I still have
no friends. No one calls. No one asks me to come over.

The young students I teach are mostly eager
to learn, to listen, sometimes pity me,
as when I told them, I don't have a car.
One brought me a miniature Cadillac.

The period between my hair dyeing has been
shortened, still no husband, no kids. No one to come
home to. No one to cook my favorite dishes for.
With winter ahead when all nature will be asleep,

or be dead, I refuse to take pictures of things
not worth seeing. I'll just write them, about where I live.
I have moved upward into a two-bedroom apartment
in a building, but motel-like, called Uptown Apartments,

near Tait's Supermarket, Frederick's Coffee House
and World Gifts, two minutes away, in front of which
my first Saturday here, I witnessed the joyful dancing
of Bosnian Muslims. I've never gone back there again.

Upstairs my landlady, Barbara Lane, lives
with her old daughter. I have a dishwasher now.
I love stacking my dirty dishes! I push a button
and water cascades over them, over my life—

without change, day to day. I hardly write letters anymore,
even to my friends. At the office we email each other,
as we can't seem to walk two doors down, to say what we have
to say. I don't take pictures, nor arrange old photos in albums.

Mercury, "Friendship 7"

in memoriam John H. Glenn, Jr. (1921–2016)

One year after my birth, three times
John Glenn orbited the Earth in five
hours seventeen minutes. He was too
valuable then as the first American to do so,
but as if a has-been, he was then suddenly retired
three years later. Sworn in as Ohio senator,
he served his country for twenty-four years,
then broke another record at age seventy-seven years,
as the oldest man to fly in space, six months
and four days, as a *Discovery* crew member.
As a hobby he collected sunsets, as if heaven.
He said he loved watching them from space, now
remembering. A fearless, quiet man, who stayed
away from the glitz, he preferred the sun's rays.

Traveling on a Train to Paris

In the middle of a harvested wheatfield
strewn with golden bales, two deer run as if
on a tapestry like the ones we saw

at the Tapestry Museum in Aix-en-Provence...
Even on the train to Paris, we can smell the wet wheatfields
on which cows and occasional sheep graze

after a storm, a gentle rain in the worst heat wave in decades.
We pass sunflower fields, Van Gogh–like, then the thin trees
in occasional old villages, around castles and churches.

Then the factories, electric windmills, high-wire poles,
roads leading to who knows where... While above us
sunrays emerge from the clouds—too short a respite.

Getting Ready for Parades

       Mardi Gras '98

Already the streetcar has stopped running,
yet the tours still continue, with horse-drawn
carriages carrying tourists privately,
past the Garden District mansions,
the drivers telling them stories of those who
once lived in these plantation houses on St. Charles.
But once the parades start, all traffic stops.

The same white homeless couple
I saw from the Louisiana bus months ago
are now selling cotton candy. Along
St. Charles in the rain, on wooden slats,
the Mardi Gras–colored candy
hangs in bags, covered by plastic.

While seagulls form a V in the sky,
so do the NOPD Officers in cars dressed in blue
in front of the two rented buses marked
with the crescent and star—here at Mardi Gras
Parade Headquarters, parked in front
of Schoen Funeral Parlor. They exit the cars,
in their blue shirts, and black pants—
ready for the evening parade.
A few hang at Fat Harry's warming up
inside, away from the February drizzle.

Out-of-towners going to the parade arrive in
crazy pink outfits, wearing wigs, and all kinds
of beads they purchased in the French Quarter,
as if they won't catch any more throws tonight.
Parade goers, whose Uptown parade won't be
canceled tonight, carry coolers with drinks.

Last night we went to hear Brooks and Baraka
reading in honor of Black History month,
"The only month they allow us to work,"
Baraka lamented. I won't go to the parades,
but to work early, before the streetcar
stops running during the parades, but also
an excuse not to look at the Marquis de Sade
and his Uptown friends he never introduced.

Carnival Time in New Orleans

Clearly, it has to stop. Visitors are perplexed
or disgusted by beads in trees, broken cups,
filth on our streets which we love to collect
quickly, this parade garbage. We who all love
the Krewe d'État parade's perverse costumes,
the flashy, blinking necklaces the women
throw from Muses, claim it all as ours.
We stomp on doubloons we love to collect.
We rush to Zulu to catch coconuts, in glitter,
standing in the sun until we get sunburnt.

The throws pile up, parade by parade.
How many stuffed animals does our son
want to cuddle? How many swords, spears,
and tri-colored umbrellas, purple, green
and gold—the Mardi Gras colors—can he adore?
It has to stop! Night rolls get crazy, sexy adults
showering faces of flambeaux carriers with pennies,
nickels, dimes (though they prefer bills).
The crews bring famous people to throw
plastic beads, toys: Kevin Costner, Glenn Close,
Nicholas Cage, King of Bacchus. Bare-breasted
women scream, "Throw me something, mister!"

We read out wicked signs of the themed parades,
laugh with men, or not, in wigs, costumed, faces
masked, painted, in drag. We dance at parties,
we gulp red beans and rice, jambalaya, King Cake
with embedded baby. If you bite into it, you have
the party next year, lunatics you don't know.
We rock for Endymion, the biggest triple-decker
floats—only one parade rolling Mid-City since Katrina.
It's always my birthday this time of the year,
I have everything to celebrate. At the end

we drag loot home, sick stuff we can't use,
throws we give away to those who visit,
strangers or friends, the rest of the year and after.
Midnight. Ash Wednesday.

4
CALLED BY NAMES

Ad Infinitum

A hundred years ago in the twenties the Red Army torched
Orthodox churches in Moscow. In the eighties they tore down

Lenin, Stalin, Marx statutes, even Engels's
after the Berlin wall came down.

Ordinary Iraqis tore down huge Hussein statues
in Baghdad after the second Gulf War, after

the U.S. troops barged in. In 2001 in Afghanistan,
the Muslim Taliban soldiers tore down ancient,

third-century AD statues, priceless Buddhas.
Now militant ISIS is destroying ancient Assyrian artifacts.

They filmed themselves proudly pounding on old statues,
pillars of shrines, lions that had survived 2,000 years

in Palmyra. Their descendants vandalize, hack
to a musical background, use heavy sledgehammers

to forever erase their (and our) history of a World Heritage Site.
Now in New Orleans, the Black population led by the white

city mayor, Landrieu, want to tear down the hundred-or-so-
year-old statues of General P. G. T. Beauregard, Confederate President

Jefferson Davis, General Robert E. Lee, and others.
"Why haven't they done this a hundred years ago?" you ask.

"Why has it taken this long?" It just takes a long time sometimes.
Perhaps it is pointless to erect new statues, new monuments,

as they will surely be removed by someone in the future who simply doesn't like them, or their politics. Those who have ruled

will fall. Those who are small will rule—ad infinitum.

Voting During My Lunch Break

Displaying my driver's
license, I identify myself
to a middle-aged
Black woman who

one by one reads
the letters of my name
spelling it out for two others
to write down in a register.

I've voted here before,
at this same church
(I thought that State and
Church were supposed

to be separate, but are not),
with these same women
at this same polling place.
Yet, with my foreign name

they have a hard time
of it, laughing or, for one,
asking where I'm from,
to which I reply,

"I am an American!"
still fearful they won't
let me vote, as I was born
elsewhere, but six years

have passed since
the first time I voted.
And the candidate
actually won.

Stories of My Name

I don't like when people
        mispronounce my name,
reading the "j" as in "jar" so
        I become a/bil-john-na/:
or when, back home in Belgrade,
        they shorten it to Bilja—
because in Greece, where I
        lived as a child, I know
it means "marbles."

In India, "Billie" was my nickname,
        and in Hindi "bili ana" is "kitty, come"
or "come, kitty" (no, not "kitty cum").
        Back home, neither strange nor unusual,
my name didn't mean anything.
        It's similar to the word for
"plant" in Serbian, *biljka*. I was born
        away from Aleksinac and Niš, near
my parents' villages, not even in Serbia,
        but in North Macedonia, in Bitola,
once a metropolis with consulates,

near Ohrid, a resort town on a lake
        with the same name, its water
drawn from Biljana's springs, named
        after a legendary young woman
in a song, who is washing her clothes when
        a caravan passes. She falls in love
with its handsome leader. Because
        of the fame of this song
in all the stores in old Yugoslavia
        you could buy "Biljana" detergent.
It comes in a big blue box.
        Is there a song

or poem in America about soap? Jingles maybe?
        Does the soap's name come from a name?
Or soap from a name?

In another tale, though, the king
        of Macedonia, or Bulgaria, depending
which history you read (different countries claim him,
        a king named Samuel or Samuil)—had
a lover named Biljana. Was he the caravan leader?
        Once in Sofia, where my father worked at the embassy
in the eighties, for my birthday he bought me
        a bottle of champagne called Biljana!
Sweet, but a mystery on the American tongue,
        a name my parents didn't choose, exactly.
Following Serbian custom, after I was born
        they wrote to Dad's godparents
(the male line only counts) who gave him
        his name, whose parents gave his
father his name and back, who knows
        how many generations . . .
Their sons, little twin boys then,
        barely able to write, wrote,
on a tiny sheet of paper, in elementary school
        in Cyrillic: *Blagica, Biserka, Brankica,*
Ružica, Vesna, Vesela, Biljana, the last name
        special, me. "Dear godson, we are

delighted our goddaughters came to ask for
        a name. Now, godson, choose any one.
We'll agree to whichever you choose,
        godson. Greetings from your
godparents; we send hellos and love." They made
        me Biljana, the seventh name,
with a "B" to match my brother's Bratislav,

shortened to Bata. But please,
don't shorten my name, and don't,
I beg you, mispronounce it.
I refuse to change it to be easier
for Americans (though I admit
I'm partial to that girl, Billie Jean;
not the tennis legend, but
the dead girl in Michael Jackson's song).
Call me /Bee-lee-ahna/.

A Hierarchy of Names

      for Dušan, my nephew

My nephew says where he lives in Italy, they call
non-EU citizens *extracomunitario,* a pejorative word.
In Greece, to Italian tourists, his clients, he introduces himself
as Sean O'Brady, not Dušan Obradović, which is his real name,

and they in turn think him Irish—a good thing, not a Serb.
When the once U.S. Poet Laureate Charles Simic came to the U.S., he
changed his name from Dušan to Charles. He removed the funny mark on the c.
At the turn of the twentieth century, when a family with my last name

came through Ellis Island on their way to Omaha, Nebraska,
they changed their name to O'Bradovich, to make it Irish,
which must have been what the officers presumed it was
among the masses of starving Irish immigrating to America.

I didn't want to change my name when I became a U.S. citizen.
But I often wonder if I should have taken my husband's name
and become Billie Ann O'Gery or take his old name Dougherty
(Billie Ann O'Dougherty), very Scotch-Irish, very American?

But I'd need to keep the O to remember what used to be there,
what used to be me before I was urged to assimilate, not
to be constantly looked down upon as foreign.
In my office drawer, I keep cutouts from envelopes

addressed to me with my name misspelled and now
even get excited at the prospect of each new surprise:
Obradovie, O'Bradovic, or Biljara, Bilhana, Bilzanan or Bityana.
I did not add an h to the end of my last name. Let people struggle,

keep asking how to spell it, how to pronounce it. Perhaps my
name will become memorable. One day everyone will know

the right spelling and I won't have to do anything. Maybe some will name their children after me. Transform? Blend in?

That's the last thing I want.

You Ugly!!!

Worker fired for giving passenger a mean note
—TIMES-PICAYUNE/NEW ORLEANS ADVOCATE

I like to read the filler news, "An airport security worker in New York was fired for handing a passenger a handwritten note that said,
 'You Ugly!!!'"

In June: "Neal Strassner obtained a security video, by a public records request, and posted it on YouTube," showing her handing over the note,
 "You ugly!!!"

The passenger passed the metal detector and received this note.
To be sure he read it, the woman yelled after him to look at the note,
 "You ugly!!!"

"You gonna open the note?" she said, as he continued on to his gate.
Then, after he had read the note, she burst out laughing. It said,
 "You ugly!!!"

with not one, not two, but three exclamation points, making sure.
So, later, he complained to her bosses, as you just don't give notes like,
 "You ugly!!!"

She worked for TSA contractors (they said) and TSA has "zero tolerance for such behavior," like a kid in first grade's note to another kid saying,
 "You ugly!!!"

It is unthinkable past elementary school to behave in this manner.
We don't tell people we don't know, really, in a handwritten note,
 "You ugly!!!"

It's irrelevant if he was ugly or not. The principle is our concern.
You fat! You cripple! You smell! becomes You Black! Uglier than
 "You ugly!!!"

Who remembers manners? Does anyone teach how to be polite?
What about dignity, respect? How to speak to strangers and not say,
    "You ugly!!!"

Billie Anna thinks if a country won't teach what it knows
is right, people pass notes, they laugh as if nobody sees, or says,
    "You ugly!!!"

Latrina's Lounge,
Uptown New Orleans

The kudzu has overtaken the building,
this hairy warehouse nonetheless still stands
abandoned like TT's Eatery and Top Cat
Cleaners along the Esplanade bus route

I am taking, or Soul Brother Furniture
store off Freret on Oretha Castle Haley Blvd.
Wherever you go, down in the projects,
signs read, "Food Stamps Accepted"

only blocks away from the opulent
Garden District mansions worth millions,
gated, their blinds shut, their lawns perfect.
But here people sit in front of their houses,

waving from their steps to us on the bus.
We pass dozens of dilapidated shotgun houses
plastered with graffiti: "L.D. Slim . . .
Big George . . . MM . . ." "No Trespassing."

Rules written in code: don't enter here
or else . . . A woman next to me leans
over, nosy, to see what I am writing.
I switch to Cyrillic. A man talks to himself,

tries to light his cigarette, but then
closes his eyes, as if to nap. Babies slump
asleep on mothers' laps, their tiny heads
leaning, like ripe cantaloupes, hands up.

Freret Discount Seafood Market is closed,
Kwik Page Copy empty, so is Latrina's Lounge.
Why, I ask, would anyone choose to go
to the "Bathroom Lounge"? To wash?

To pee? Unfortunately, the name resembles
the word latrine, the bathroom lounge,
now defunct. The lady next to me looks away.
One baby starts to cry. My stop is next.

Trendsetter: Or, How I Changed India

In India as an eighteen-year-old woman,
I aspired to be a model or an actress.
So before I left, with my friend Tina
in my last few days there, we were hired to
film an ad for a factory that sold fabrics,
Bombay Dyeing. Riding a tandem bike
(as though one would ride a bike in three-inch
heels), I sat in front, she behind me, me
in white shorts with open laces on
the sides, no underwear, she in long white pants,
both of us in stilettos. Downhill
they made us ride, wildly, twenty times
to get it right for the camera, before each ride
fixing our makeup. I remembered to get
permission to take the day off school.

I thought, once I left the country, I would
never see the ad, but then ten years later
at a friend's house in Richmond, on
the far side of the planet, on PBS TV,
I caught myself on a report on advertising in India.
The reporter said how things were changing
in India, a conservative country, where
people in Bollywood movies didn't even kiss,
but now some ads even had sexual implications.
That I was *it!* I changed ads in India
in those skimpy shorts they made me wear.
I pushed the envelope. OK, so it wasn't
Playboy and I wasn't naked. But after me,
sex entered homes, movie theaters, everywhere!
Thanks to Bombay Dyeing!

Catullus's Sparrows

       a sestina for John and Petar

I heard the lemon merchant singing the song
"O Sole Mio," surrounded by tiny sparrows
looking for morsels of food beside Lake
Garda on Sirmione, while I drank a light Bardolino wine
at the Piccolo Castello, where I dined on a salad with olives,
with grilled branzino, near the castle, after a swim

in Hotel Broglia's pool in my new pink swimsuit
bought at one of the shops where a song
in Italian rose from a radio next to the long, thin olive
plate I would have bought but for the sparrow
Petar, my son, chased. We left without the Bardolino wine
I also meant to buy to drink before dinner by the lake.

Instead we strolled over a mile along the lake,
the day gorgeous, thinking maybe we would later swim
in the pool where a couple laughed drinking wine
(maybe a Bardolino), listening to songs.
I walked quietly in shade not to disturb the sparrows,
following Petar's every move, which stood on an olive

branch, while spotted swans perched beyond the olive
tree, floated alone or in pairs on the lake.
Lizardo (a lizard we named) swayed near the sparrows.
I watched him closely, aware he kept near where we'd swim,
but he was small. He'd likely be scared of me, or loud songs
swimmers sang, or clients' cars below us, near the wine

store, full of shiny bottles of grappa unlike the wines.
They also had strong pomace brandy, dipping bread, olive
oil, appetizers, digestives after dinner, music, a song,
and espresso with blue glasses in the restaurant by the lake.

The next night a macho man sped up in his fancy boat, to swim?
No way. He parked, tugged his two girlfriends like sparrows,

parading them as the crowd cheered, barely dressed sparrows,
that is, then ordered a Bardolino, the most expensive local wine,
and lit a cigarette. We watched his babes (who did not swim)
show off, swaying black necklaces, dressed in olive
silk sheaths. I thought they might fall into the lake,
tumbling over their high stilettos. A band's little song,

a song of hungry local sparrows, drifted over the lake from
the Grotte di Catullo, begging like poets for wine, for the olive
girls to dance and shine, then go before they could swim.

5
CALLED BY NATURE

The Tamed West

      at the Nebraska Fair

Buffalo Bill's bust in the Capitol in Lincoln stares
as if to haunt the few wild buffaloes left.
He tried to kill the wild, to tame the West,
but the wilderness stayed here, waiting for me:

heifers, standing beef, like large dogs, rams
dehorned, goats unlike ours back home,
horned rabbits, eyes hidden like a sheepdog's,
an Appaloosa, a paint. I saw more girls

riding horses than I'd ever seen, wished
I could ride, but the oldest were only fifteen.
Too old now, I was upset that I'd never
had a chance to ride at their age, never

saddled our famous Lipizzaner horses.
These things in my new home included
rabbits, squirrels I liked to watch, just like
the pigeons on the streets of Belgrade. They

owned the Lincoln sidewalks, lawns, and trees,
roamed wild, as everything is in the West.
Tomorrow at the market I'll buy ten ears of corn
for just a buck—it's the Cornhusker State after all.

It's the Plains. Rolling fields to horizon's end,
cowboys, boots, spurs, hats roam the city,
even today, mostly without guns. They don't
want to be missed. They love loud, sexy,

bleached-blond women, gas-hog trucks in bright colors.
They live for bloody rodeos, dehorning heifers,
big families, small bars, myth-webbed outcasts.
My girlfriend says the cosmos is all lies riding

against us, that appearances may be dreams.
Can't we look at life as it is now, open-minded,
here, where some buffalo still stand in
the wild by the highways like ghost figures?

I have passed them, smelled them, tasted them—
giants. Nothing has changed, maybe, not even
the cowgirl who says, "You have to be intuitive,
or get broken. Welcome to the Wild West!"

Scenes at the Sheldon Art Gallery

I.

On the ground, bricks are laid parallel, or
perpendicular, touch, with a half inch of sand filling
in between. Sand sometimes covers red and dark
brown bricks, so do occasional parts of leaves, cigarette
butts, pieces of glass, so minute, they'd be unseen

without the sun illuminating them for us,
sparkling like lost powdered diamonds.
Cemented tiny rocks stuck together, it seems,
until the end of eternity—their color here
dominantly beige, like the ground, or people,

with occasional dark spots, black rocks standing
alone. A boot imprint on the sand reminds me
of the marks astronauts made on the moon.
But no one here is looking at these,
the sun shining on them so brightly, no one

except me, sitting, almost in pain,
heat on my buttocks, where my black pants
absorb light, my white sweater's a nuisance—
like snow in Louisiana. I try to adapt.
From a nearby tree a student calls out,

a light wind blowing her hair, leaves falling.
She tells me how once for Paul Simon's concert, she
climbed a tree in Central Park, so now here as well.
Bending the branch, pen, paper clutched, she
throws her bag to the ground, climbs down, goes.

II.

Why have I never noticed white signs with blue
wheelchair "hangman" characters? Or arrows

pointing where wheelchair access can go?
In front of the Sheldon Art Gallery people
are told they can't climb the stairs. No wheelchairs.

They have to go through the side doors the way
Black people used to pass through back doors.
How lucky I am to be able to walk up
seven steps, landing, five steps, landing, I'm in!
I brush off a tiny green fly waiting on my paper.

Not thinking I hurt it, but have I killed it?
No! She's back. Stop bothering me! I blow her away.
A black butterfly flutters with his wings
roaming around white flowers on the green bush
enjoying his life, maybe his single day—yet

so much to experience! He feels no tomorrow,
no yesterday. I watch and think we don't forget
ourselves to touch this, touch that, going
to work . . . for what? A new car, a TV
to see what I sit here spending my life to know?

Already the shadows in front of the people who pass,
leaning to say it's 2:00 p.m., each leaning
lower, a little burdened, trees dropping
shade like the 2:00 p.m. hand my watch holds.
This is how the day dies. So I look around. Now.

Nature Unleashed

    for M.

Living on different continents, my friend and I,
he from Sudan, in Africa, I from New Orleans,
hope to meet soon in our native city Belgrade.
Yet a sandstorm has begun there. Planes may not fly.
Nature unleashed herself, unexpectedly, her choice.
Sahara Desert storms get violent, red sand grains
go all the way to the Acropolis or even Big Ben.
Who knows if he'll even be able to leave now.

When from Europe I wanted to fly
back to the States, ash from a volcano in Iceland
swelled so thick air traffic control feared
it would damage aircraft engines, so they closed
huge areas of air space to traffic. But skies cleared
so I flew. I also made it OK from the States
to Serbia this year, coming down like a duck
into endless rain, the worst floods since the first

weather records 140 years ago. Before I landed
(after flying twenty-one hours, changing flights
in three airports seemingly as big as some countries),
I saw only fields of wheat skidding under me,
water-soaked, but no farmer tending what
should be ripened. It looked like Louisiana,
near the swamps where I live. I felt like a traveler
in an ancient boat coming up from a rocking keel.

Then, on the ground, as we crossed a bridge,
we watched our cab driver glare at Sava River's
soaked sandbags on its banks, the mud swirls
turned by the sun into blood. But it was quiet
like my computer when, jet lagged, online
at 2:00 a.m., my friend in Sudan appeared

on Skype. He was taking a break, getting away
from feeding refugees in camps not getting away

from wars, famine, drought, last crops sun-cooked
to crumble like old leaves. Beneath them, the ground
cracked, open like a mouth to swallow them. My friend
who had worked thirty years for the UNHCR, the last
year before retirement beating him like the winds,
"Just lucky," he said, five hours before he was to leave
for Belgrade. He'd been away a long time.
I send good vibes, wait. But nature unleashed
herself on her own impulse, not caring who he'd see—
Serbian flooding disaster, or Louisiana's coastline
vanishing, winds, flooding in New Orleans, my city,
people smothered by an ooze of not just water, from
Hurricane Katrina drowning, breaking the levees.
We want beauty. We have to learn to see; no one wants
the blue tarps covering roofs, wind-shredded trees,
the invisible mold rising from our bedroom walls.

At the End of the Year in the Subtropics

My son helps me to move all outside plants into the garage,
helps his father cover the plants in the ground with garbage bags
as the temperatures are going to plunge. Our papayas may die,

yet again two winters in a row. Twenty-one degrees Fahrenheit.
Worse this year than last. The papaya wilted leaves
wave their last goodbye to me. My husband finally goes to bed.

Up all night watching the water drip in the bathrooms
and kitchen, at 7:00 a.m. he turns on the dishwasher, lets the water run
in the front yard, so it doesn't freeze. He has removed the hose.

Despite the ice storm, closing I-10, the airport—New Year celebrations
continue. Our Meyer lemon dies as well. On edge all day,
my husband hears gunfire from the kitchen, thinks he left the TV on.

Katrina: My "American Pie"

Has the music in our poetry died? The poets stopped dreaming
on August 30, 2005, when Katrina hit New Orleans.
Still, we sang "American Pie," a 1971 song by Don McLean,
driving our Volkswagen Passat Wagon away. Then
the levees broke. Now I can finally see it all. Blue tarps
in Kenner shine like swimming pools from above.
Gospel music, not jazz, blares from the airport speakers,
nobody listening as if the whole place is an advertisement
for angels, Death, echoes of Hallelujahs, and "We shall
overcome." But on our radio, the song continued to play live.

At the Alamo rental, forty days and forty nights after the storm,
when we were allowed to return, we see a huge fallen tree
that stands behind the sign "midsize." Some damage on the
way Uptown, no streetcar on St. Charles. No traffic lights
three streets toward the lake from St. Charles, only yanked
wires, four-way stop signs. Then appear lines of water
risen on buildings, the stink, the piles of rotting furniture,
appliances, drywall in front of the houses people have
gotten to already, as the rest remain silent. In our neighborhood,

Mid-City, flooded midway, above trashcan level,
every house has markers, luckily most with 0/zeros
for the number of dead inside. In front of Robért's
Fresh Market, the last store I had gone to before evacuating
that Saturday to buy fruit and dry milk, now stands
a huge mound of junk. We turn on to the street with
O'Malley House where we held our wedding party—
it looks beaten. Through heaped refrigerators, washing
machines, furniture, we take Banks. Suddenly the huge
sign on Mona's restaurant lights up, as if this minute,

seeing me after eighty days, has made it excited.
We veer then onto our street, S. Scott. Quiet among

the rubble is the house. I'm not afraid of what I'll see inside.
I'm prepared. John, his brother Michael, friends had gone inside
forty days ago, removed the soggy books, the carpets,
the destroyed bookshelves, furniture, Petar's toys,
the appliances, all in front of the house, poor trash.
I go around it, look at the broken windows from three
storms that visited us, Cindy, Katrina, Rita, three furies,
scarring us this summer. The garage slumps over John's old car.

Some still alive, my plants hang on, despite no rain for months.
Alley cats, miraculously survived, come out. "Hello!"
They, too, greet me. I take them inside, no food, no electricity
but running water! We must get out before the dark.
I find pots from my kitchen in the garbage—they're fine.
I lift them, who threw them out? Why? I'll wash them.
In the backyard, ladder, bar stools, metal chairs—all good.
We lug them into the house, tarp them, leave the kitchen
furniture outside. Inside is a bad story—walls, four feet up
neatly cut from the floor, mold specks still rising. Cabinets

stripped, everything is exposed. I see through the bathroom—
living room from back to front, and through the kitchen—dining room.
Under more tarps our downstairs furniture gathers like ghosts.
Upstairs seems OK, boxes, books, from downstairs moved up.
On the porch scattered moldy books crowd together
like old friends. We welcome them back in—so what if they're
damaged, mold turning their shells? What's inside them
can't be bought. I lift them, one by one. They cannot be
redeemed, only kept. Can we make sense of what's gone?
What do we do with them—like memories of Serbia, England, China?

John will oil the legs of chairs and tables to look new.
The piano I bought John can't be saved. Soon days blur.
Our rug man calls back, says, "Dry outside, fold, bring to me."

"How much to save?" I ask. "If a dead body was in it,
six dollars per foot then, otherwise two." "No dead body,"
I say. But what do we pay for my parents' worn, soggy
carpets, the Turkish rug, our wedding gift from John's family,
or the one from his Russian grandmother? It's just a story
we became part of, one to tell on holidays when we can see
our son happily playing with his new toys, waving, "Bye, bye."

Raccoon in the Garbage

Huddled like a fuzzy ball
on some old, wet newspapers
in a bottom corner of the garbage can,
he lies hoping not to be detected.

But the thunk of my garbage bag
falling opposite startles him,
so as to lift his pointed nose,
his sleepy eyes just enough
to see who dares wake him up.

At first, I thought he was the stray
gray cat who meows by my doorstep
each day (my landlady feeds him there).
When I saw his long face, I stared back,
and as if to a long-lost friend, said,

"Good morning!" as he rolled over,
among the potato peels and melon rinds,
then went back to sleep.

Waiting for Papayas

Placed in a pot, the papaya seeds from store-bought fruit
grew into a giant tree in just four months—we noticed
after our brief European trip. The tree hovered over the tomato
and basil, blocking the sun from them, its wide leaves
like an umbrella shielding the dwarves below.

Curious passersby began to stop, to look at it by our driveway,
in disbelief, as if hungry wolves, eager for the fruit to ripen.
Like tennis fans they gaped awaiting each ball to drop, straight
down the line. A flow of visitors passed by, but the forty or
more papayas took their time from April to December, before the frost.

Finally, from the ripe papayas, I made papaya jam,
designed a label with my son and gave jars of jam
to his teachers, friends, family and colleagues for
Christmas. Everyone loved the papaya jam, even wanted
to order more. We thought of starting to sell until

the winter days grew darker, colder. The skies turned gray.
Everyone got sick, and sneezed. Concerned about possible frost,
I cut the large unripe fruit off to use for stews. Then it snowed
for two days, and full of forty fruits, the tree froze. We cut
the tree down, threw the rest of the football-like fruit into the trash.

How could I have grown such a huge papaya tree from a seed?
If only all the fruit could have ripened before the frost . . . So
abundant it was, we could share it with our neighbor
who'd been grateful for its shade on her front porch, and now
we all lament, how so much came so soon from so little.

Yellow Water Lily

> Everywhere you go will be somewhere
> You've never been.
> —NATASHA TRETHEWEY

Nymphaea Species Mix, leaf in water;
some leaves stick out, strong stems,
but most lie on the surface of the water
like small disheveled bodies, legs, arms

embraced, sun reflecting on them, power
from above. Water marries the rainbow shades,
dirt, dead flies float in filthy green
ooze, a huge orange goldfish gulps

as if grasped by *Eichhornia crassipes*
(water hyacinth). Small birds cry out,
wanting attention from mates, rivals. I sit
at the concrete sculpture garden's heart,

practically a stem of the bushes in plant pots.
A passerby looks on, hands in pockets,
curious to know what I'm doing.
In the distance sirens blare, fire trucks racing too,

like rabbits in fear from, fire. Whose house?
The heat forces me to stay still in shade.
Beside me a sleeping statue suddenly arises,
jacket in hand, palm up. I see it is goodbye,

his Nebraskan granddad, ball cap on to save
weathered skin, his body now rested, needs
to go somewhere. But I sit, wanting the full
story, by a black statue, wishbone-shaped,

rough, metal lifted over scarred cement.
A plane drags by loud, drones closer, goes
off, out of sight, as if never there.
An oak, its leaves limp, seems to point. Light

brown branches, like old uniforms, remind me
how things change. Boys take photos, one couple
makes shy statue love, nearly eternal,
their steel fingers open, cradling dead daisies.

Wind touches my hair, day-tangled, hard
to brush, or comb, too long to pull back,
waving wildly, like the brownish
crawl of prairie grass dancing to its own rhythm.

Instead of crows I think I hear, I spot nearby a woman
pushing a carriage reassuring the baby
crying inside. No crows today. Cold is coming,
nudging the tree shade, too, plants closing.

Through the weave of my sweater, I sense
even ants crawling into sidewalk cracks, doors
maybe. I glance at my watch. Too long
out? I'll grab a lily, then run to catch the bus.

NOTES

"The Dream That Keeps Returning"—*Bera* is a Hindi term for a waiter. *Biryani* is an Indian dish made with highly seasoned rice and meat, fish, or vegetables.

"Spiritual Baptism"—Ganesh is the Hindu elephant god. Ganesh Chaturthi falls between 22 August and 20 September every year. This Hindu festival celebrates the arrival of Ganesh to earth from Kailash Parvat with his mother Goddess Parvati/Gauri. The festival is marked with the installation of Ganesh clay idols privately in homes, or publicly on elaborate pandals (temporary stages). The festival ends on the tenth day after start, when the idol is immersed in the sea. In Mumbai alone, around 150,000 statues are immersed annually; the clay idol dissolves and Ganesh is believed to return to Mount Kailash to Parvati and Shiva. The festival celebrates Lord Ganesh as the god of New Beginnings and the Remover of Obstacles as well as the god of wisdom and intelligence and is observed throughout India.

"Pickled Snake in Wine"—Stanza 4, line 1 is from Salman Rushdie's *Midnight's Children* (Random House, 2006), 119 (originally published in 1981 by Jonathan Cape).

"*Ενοικιαζεται* (For Rent)"—*Τράπεζες* is Greek for banks.

"Taking Pictures in Des Moines"—This poem was written during the civil war in Yugoslavia between Serbs, Croats, and Bosnian Muslims. Although I am an American citizen, ethnically I am still a Serb.

"Latrina's Lounge, Uptown New Orleans"—*Lavatrina* means to wash. Latrine is a toilet, especially a communal one in a camp or barracks.

"Trendsetter: Or, How I Changed India"—The reader may consult the Bombay Dyeing ad on YouTube, "Dressed to Kill, Old Doordashan ad": https://www.youtube.com/watch?v=rEUFqn1gOnE.

"The Tamed West"—Lipizzaner horses—a beautiful white breed of horses from the town of Lipica in Slovenia, formerly Yugoslavia.

"Katrina: My 'American Pie'" was inspired by "American Pie," a 1971 song by Don McLean. In the song he drives a Chevy to the levee instead of the type of car we drove, a Volkswagen Passat.

ABOUT THE AUTHOR

Biljana D. Obradović is a Serbian-American poet, translator, critic, and Professor of English at Xavier University of Louisiana in New Orleans, where she has been part of the Southern literary scene for almost three decades. She has published four collections of poems (*Le Riche Monde*, *Frozen Embraces*, *Little Disruptions*, and *Incognito*) and three books of translations from Serbian into English and five from English into Serbian. She has also edited two anthologies, as well as the *Atlanta Review* issue on Serbia, and a book of essays.

She grew up in Yugoslavia, Greece, and India. She received an MFA in Creative Writing (Poetry) from Virginia Commonwealth University and a PhD in English from the University of Nebraska, Lincoln. She was awarded the Rastko Petrović Award for her second collection, *Frozen Embraces*; the Miša Djordjević Book Prize for *Cat Painters: An Anthology of Contemporary Serbian Poetry*, mostly translated by her, and coedited with Dubravka Djurić; and the North American Society for Serbian Studies (NASSS) Book Prize (formerly Mihajlo Miša Djordjević Book Prize) for her translation of Dubravka Djurić's *The Politics of Hope (After the War): Selected and New Poems*. She has also been honored with an Honorary Citizenship of Nebraska, the Norman C. Francis Award for Research from Xavier University of Louisiana, and the Masaryk Academy of Arts Medal for Artistic Achievements from the Czech Republic. Her work has been translated into Serbian, Italian, Korean, Chinese, and Japanese.

www.ingramcontent.com/pod-product-compliance
Lightning Source LLC
Chambersburg PA
CBHW031124160426
43192CB00008B/1100